Easy to Play Guitar Trios

Franco Bertucci

To access the online audio recording go to:
WWW.MELBAY.COM/30801MEB

Cover guitar images are the Grand Concert Cedar Brazilian, Grand Concert Blanca, Auditorium New Mexico Cutaway by Pimentel Guitars, Albuquerque, New Mexico, USA.

WWW.MELBAY.COM

Introduction

I did not intend to become a guitar teacher but a few years ago I found myself teaching guitar to a jumbled mix of complete beginners, novices and intermediate players—often in the same room at the same time. I was surprised by how much I enjoyed it.

Performing music in a traveling band had been quite fun, but the new thrill of hearing a young student play a simple melody, clearly and without affectation, took me by surprise. It was like discovering music all over again. Of course, teaching can be tedious but my students made me hear the most humdrum and familiar music with new ears.

Still, I had a hard time finding music that my students of different levels could learn and play together without boring the more advanced, nor frustrating the beginners.

I began to arrange some of my favorite songs and melodies in three parts so that I would have some material to use in my classes. I wrote easy, medium and hard parts in each piece so that all my students could handle at least one of the parts, even though some of them had just begun and some had pretty fast fingers.

Like my classes, these arrangements are a jumbled mix. I never have been a specialist in any genre. What the pieces have in common are good melodies that I happen to like and are playable by intermediate and less accomplished guitarists. I have arranged these tunes in easy guitar keys, using open strings as much as possible.

Several of the first and second parts in these pieces will be challenging even for intermediate students. That is good. They need it. Most of the melodic parts are pretty easy and rewardingly quick to learn. The third, or low part is extremely simple in most cases.

When I teach these pieces, I sometimes play one of the written parts; other times I accompany the class and keep time by strumming or fingerpicking the chords. I have included the chord progressions for most of the pieces. Occasionally I assign a student to complement the arrangement using the chord symbols.

Whether you are a teacher or beginning student, I hope you enjoy these little pieces as much as I have.

Sincerely,
Franco Bertucci

P.S. The first and second guitar parts in this book are largely playable on any soprano instrument, such as the violin, flute or recorder. (Sometimes a guitar class must take in strays.)

Contents

Traditional Melodies

Classical Melodies

Original Melodies

Note on the Recordings

Most of these recordings were made with a Martin D-15 guitar and a little, handheld Tascam digital recorder in my music studio during a rainy winter in the Pacific Northwest. If you listen closely, you may be able to hear the rain on the roof in a few of the tracks.

Traditional Melodies

Am Yisrael Chai

This very catchy tune can be played with only two fingers, though some students will try to get away with using only their fast first finger. Don't let them.

2
The Banshee
Irish reel
arr. by Franco Bertucci
With a will
Guitar 1
Guitar 2
Guitar 3
G C D G C G Em D
Gtr. 1
Gtr. 2
Gtr. 3
G C D G C G Em D
Am C Em
Am C Em C G Em D G

Hey Ho, Nobody Home

16th Century English round
arranged by Franco Bertucci

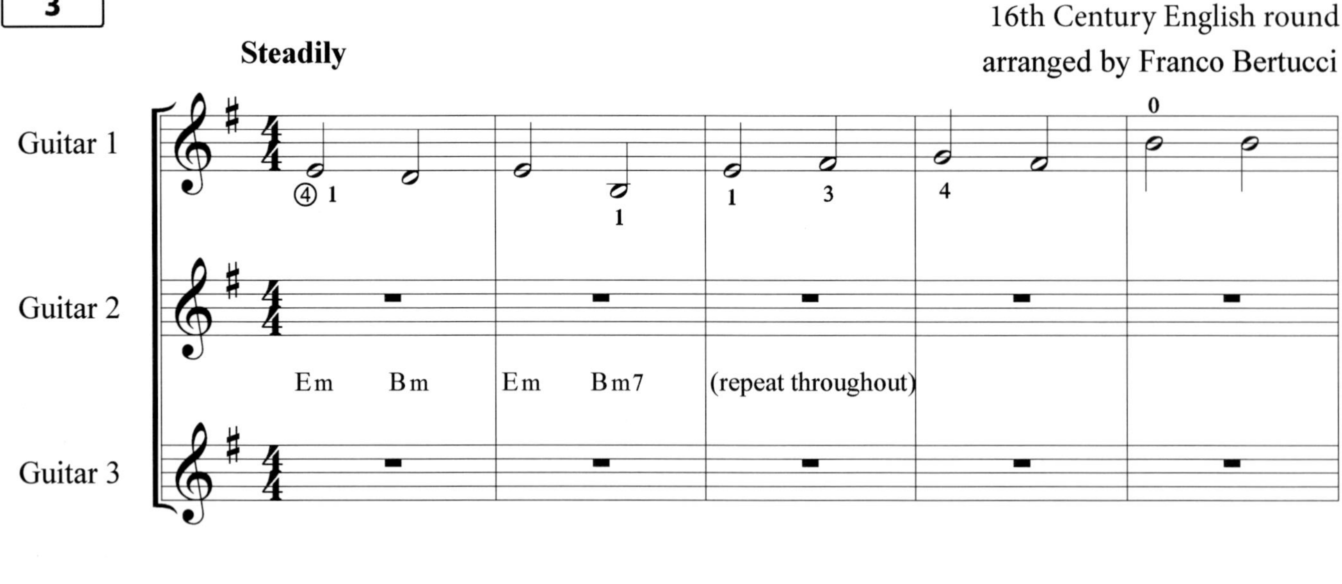

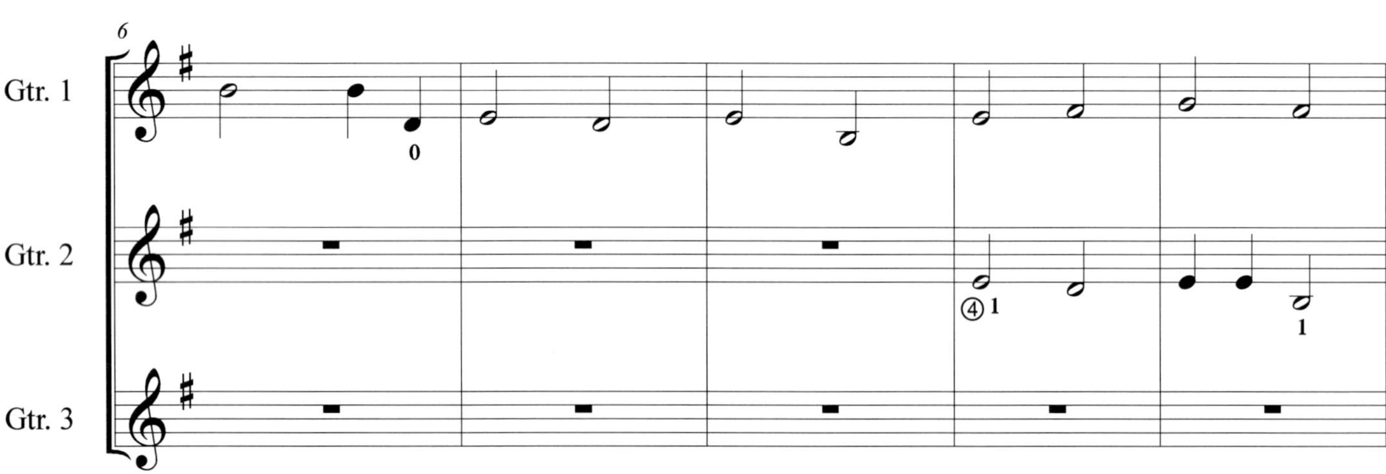

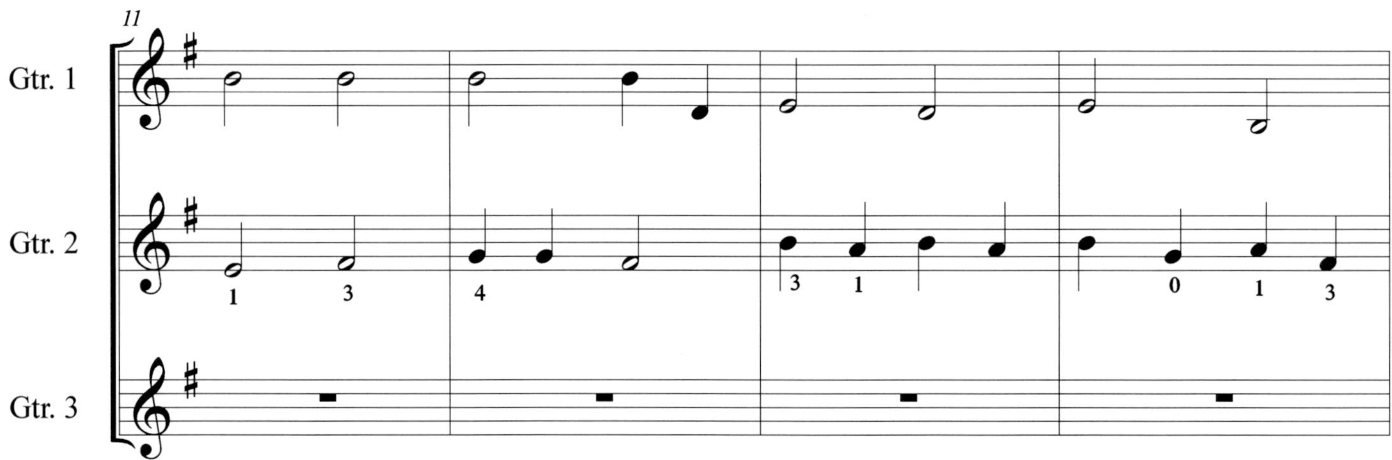

This piece is really a round of six bars. The simplest thing you can do is to use only the first six measures of the first guitar part. Each succeeding player waits two bars to begin.

15
Gtr. 1
Gtr. 2
Gtr. 3
④ 1
1
1
19
Gtr. 1
Gtr. 2
Gtr. 3
1
3
4
3
1
0
3
23
Gtr. 1
Gtr. 2
Gtr. 3

27
Gtr. 1
Gtr. 2
Gtr. 3
31
0
② 3
0
Gtr. 1
Gtr. 2
Gtr. 3
33
2
3
3
Gtr. 1
0
② 3
0
Gtr. 2
Gtr. 3

This page has been left blank to avoid an awkward page turn.

Korobushka

I learned from students that this tune is used in the enormously popular video game, *Tetris*. I first learned it from my guitar teacher as a teenager.

13
Gtr. 1
Gtr. 2
Gtr. 3
17
Gtr. 1
Gtr. 2
Gtr. 3
21
Gtr. 1
Gtr. 2
Gtr. 3

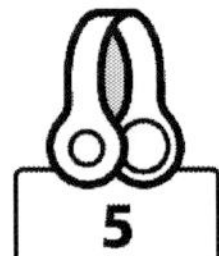

Julia Delaney

Irish reel
arranged by Franco Bertucci

Lively

Guitar 1
Guitar 2
Guitar 3

Dm | C Dm | Dm

Gtr. 1
Gtr. 2
Gtr. 3

4

Am | Dm | C Dm

Gtr. 1
Gtr. 2
Gtr. 3

7

1. 2.

Dm | Am Dm | Am Dm

10
Gtr. 1
Gtr. 2
Gtr. 3
Dm
C
Dm
13
Gtr. 1
Gtr. 2
Gtr. 3
Am
Dm
C
D.C. al Fine
16
Gtr. 1
Gtr. 2
Gtr. 3
Dm
Am
Dm

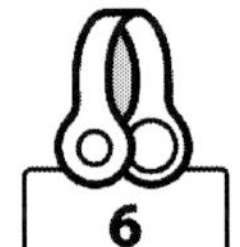

Santa Lucia

Neopolitan song
arranged by Franco Bertucci

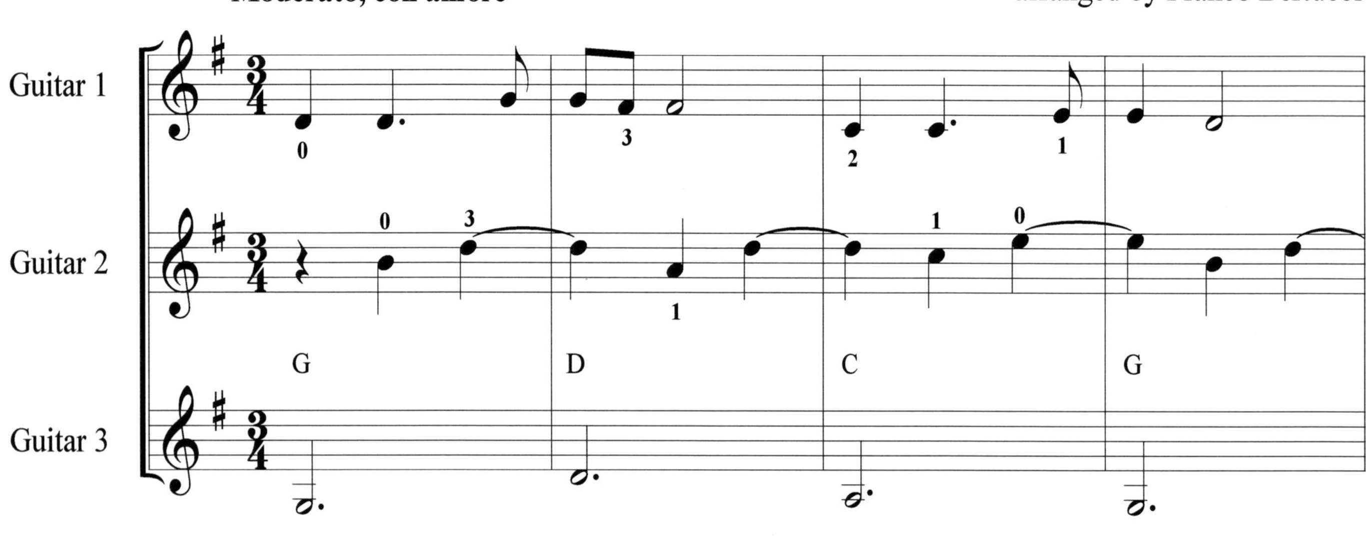

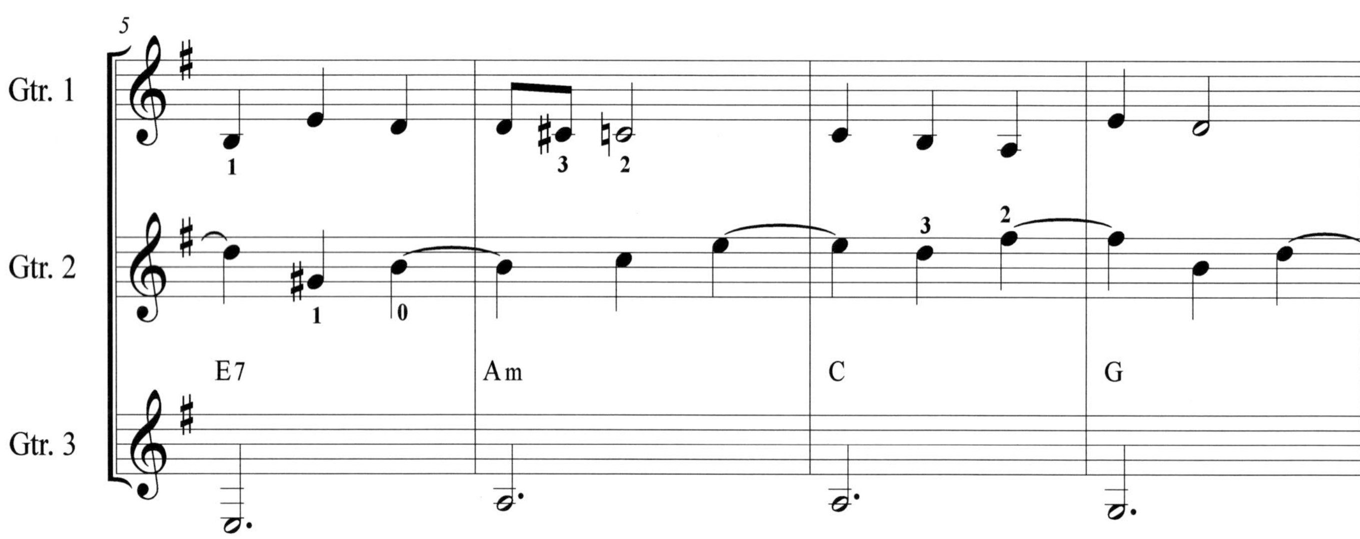

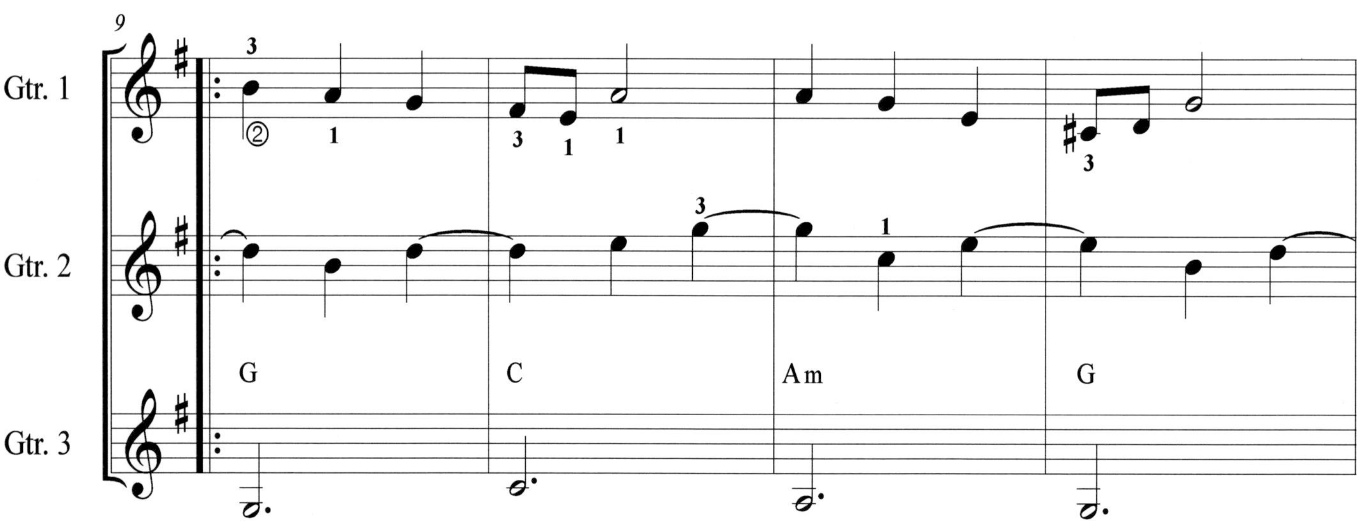

Although it comes from Italy, this melody may be more popular in Scandinavia. I first learned this song in order to play it for a fellow teacher's Swedish class and their "Sankta Lucia" festival.

13
1.
Gtr. 1
Gtr. 2
G
Am
D
G
Gtr. 3
17
2.
Gtr. 1
Gtr. 2
D
G
Gtr. 3

Scarborough Fair

English folk song
arranged by Franco Bertucci

Wistfully ♩ = 108

Guitar 1

Guitar 2

Am G Am

Guitar 3

5

Gtr. 1

Gtr. 2

Am G Am C

Gtr. 3

10

Gtr. 1

Gtr. 2

F Am D Am

Gtr. 3

15
Gtr. 1
Gtr. 2
Gtr. 3
3
1
0
0
2
0
2
3
C
Em
Am
19
Gtr. 1
Gtr. 2
Gtr. 3
G
Em
Am
G
23
Gtr. 1
Gtr. 2
Gtr. 3
0
Em
G
Am

Skye Boat Song

Scottish song
arr. by Franco Bertucci

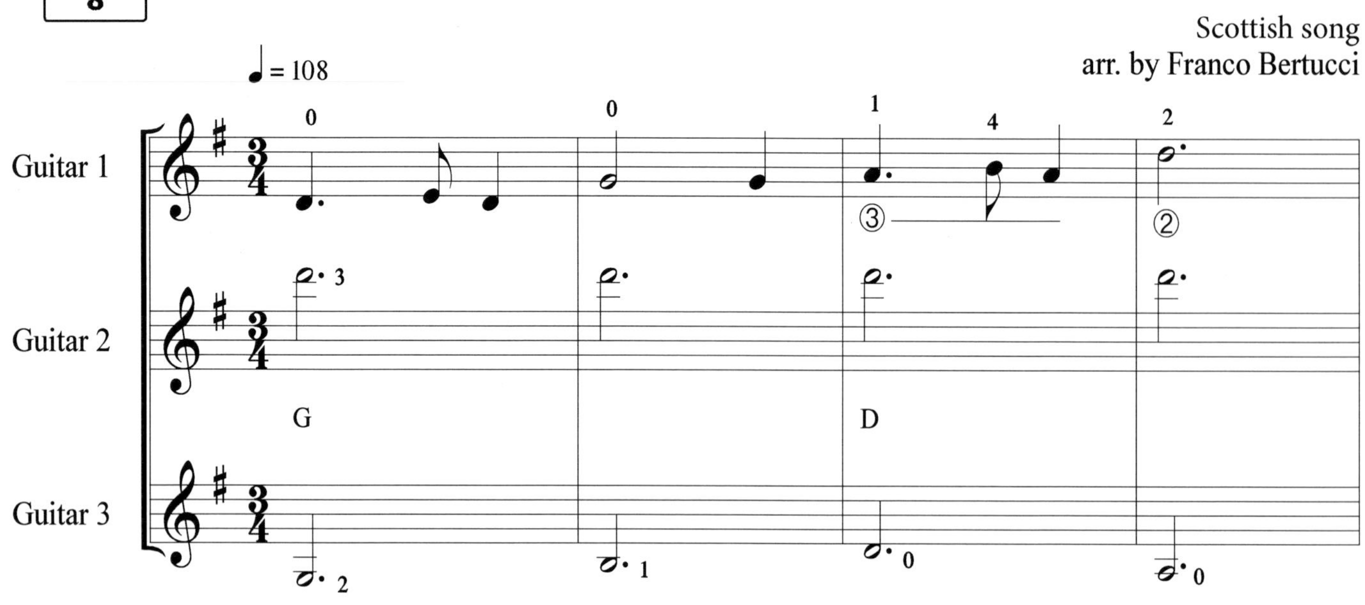

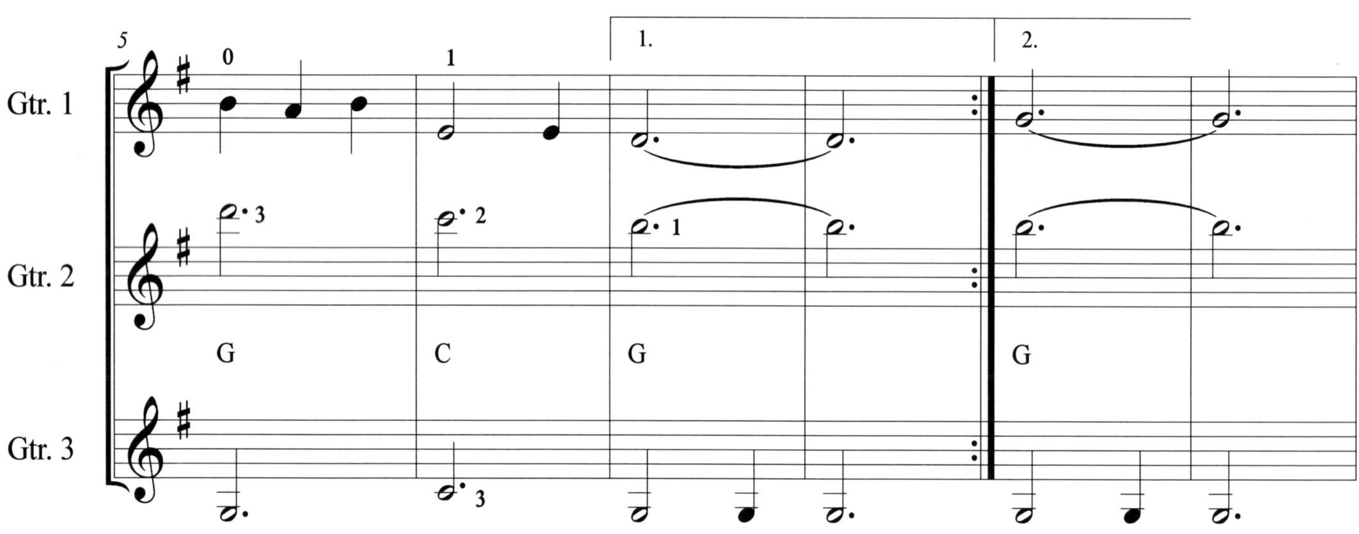

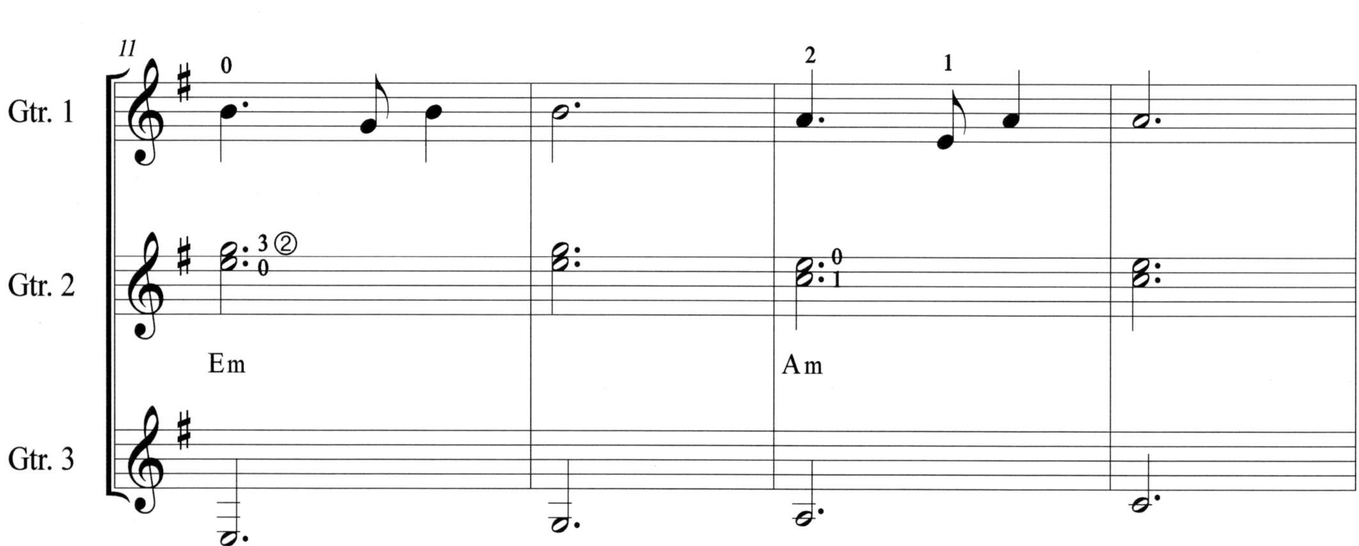

15
Gtr. 1
Gtr. 2
Gtr. 3
0
0
Em
19
Gtr. 1
Gtr. 2
Gtr. 3
Am
23
Gtr. 1
Gtr. 2
Gtr. 3
Em
D

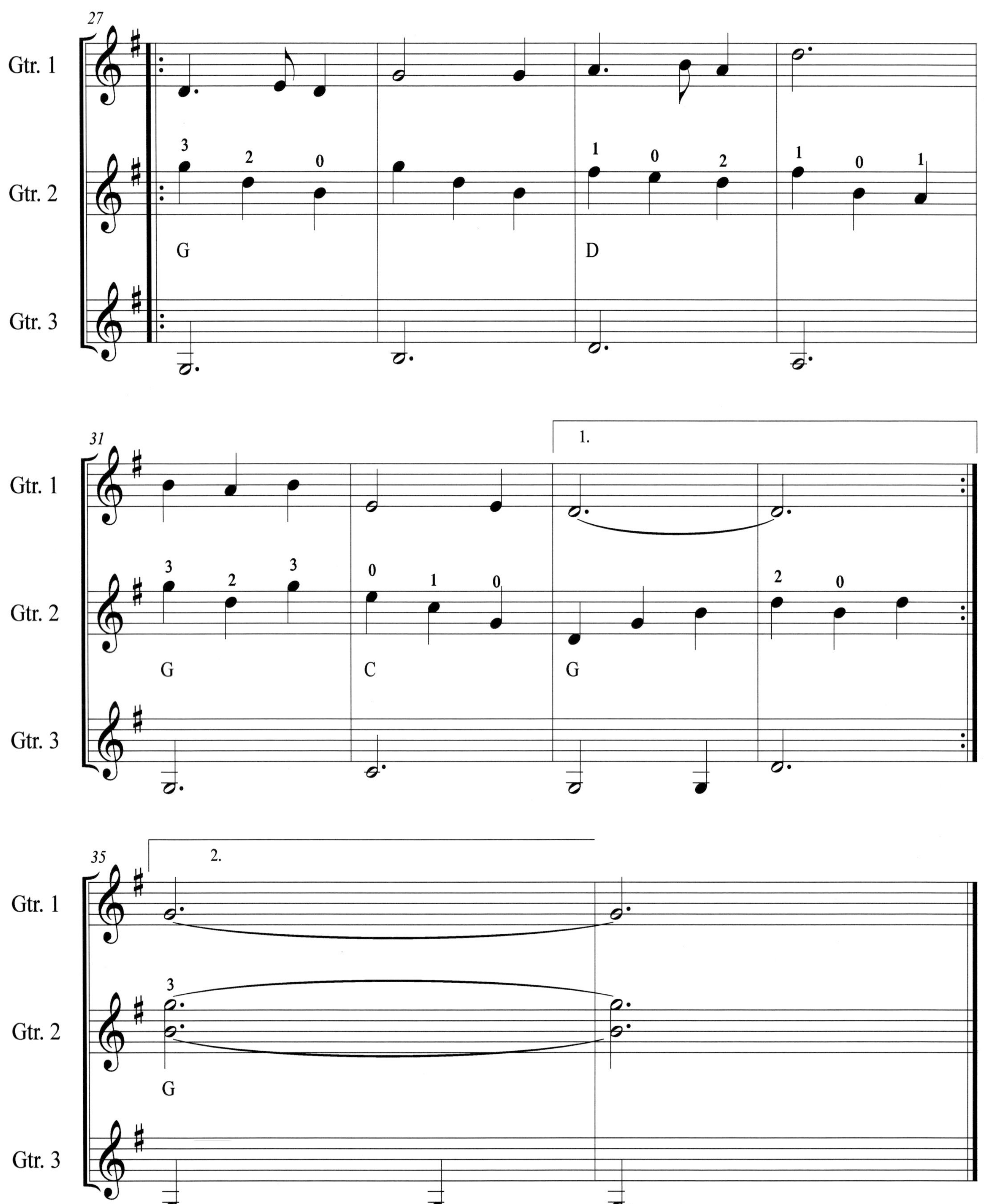
27
Gtr. 1
Gtr. 2
Gtr. 3
G
D
31
1.
C
35
2.

Classical Melodies

Canon in G for Three Guitars

Pachelbel
arranged by Franco Bertucci

Guitar 1
Guitar 2
Guitar 3

G D Em Bm

5
Gtr. 1
Gtr. 2
Gtr. 3

C G C D

9
Gtr. 1
Gtr. 2
Gtr. 3

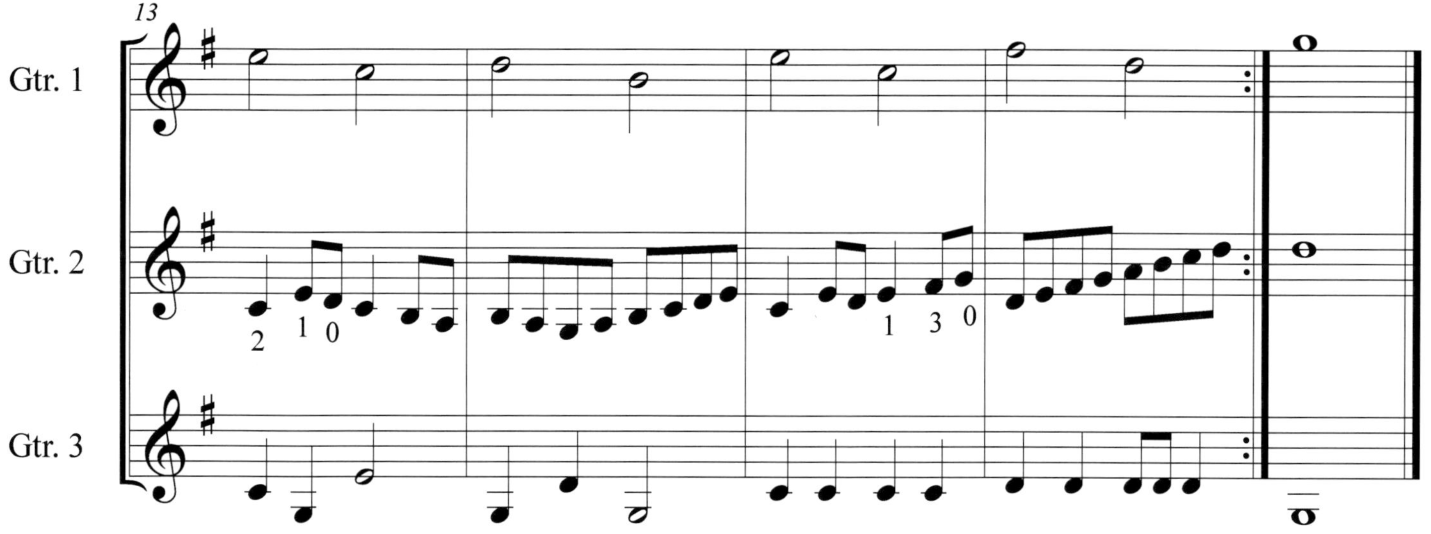
13
Gtr. 1
Gtr. 2
2 1 0
1 3 0
Gtr. 3

The middle part is challenging but this part of the sonata is very effective as a guitar trio. This has been a hit at recitals.

9
Gtr. 1
Gtr. 2
Gtr. 3
11
Gtr. 1
Gtr. 2
Gtr. 3
13
Gtr. 1
Gtr. 2
Gtr. 3
15
Gtr. 1
Gtr. 2
Gtr. 3

Some of my students learn to play this simple, lovely melody on their very first day of guitar class.

Original Melodies

Dow Now

Groovily

Franco Bertucci

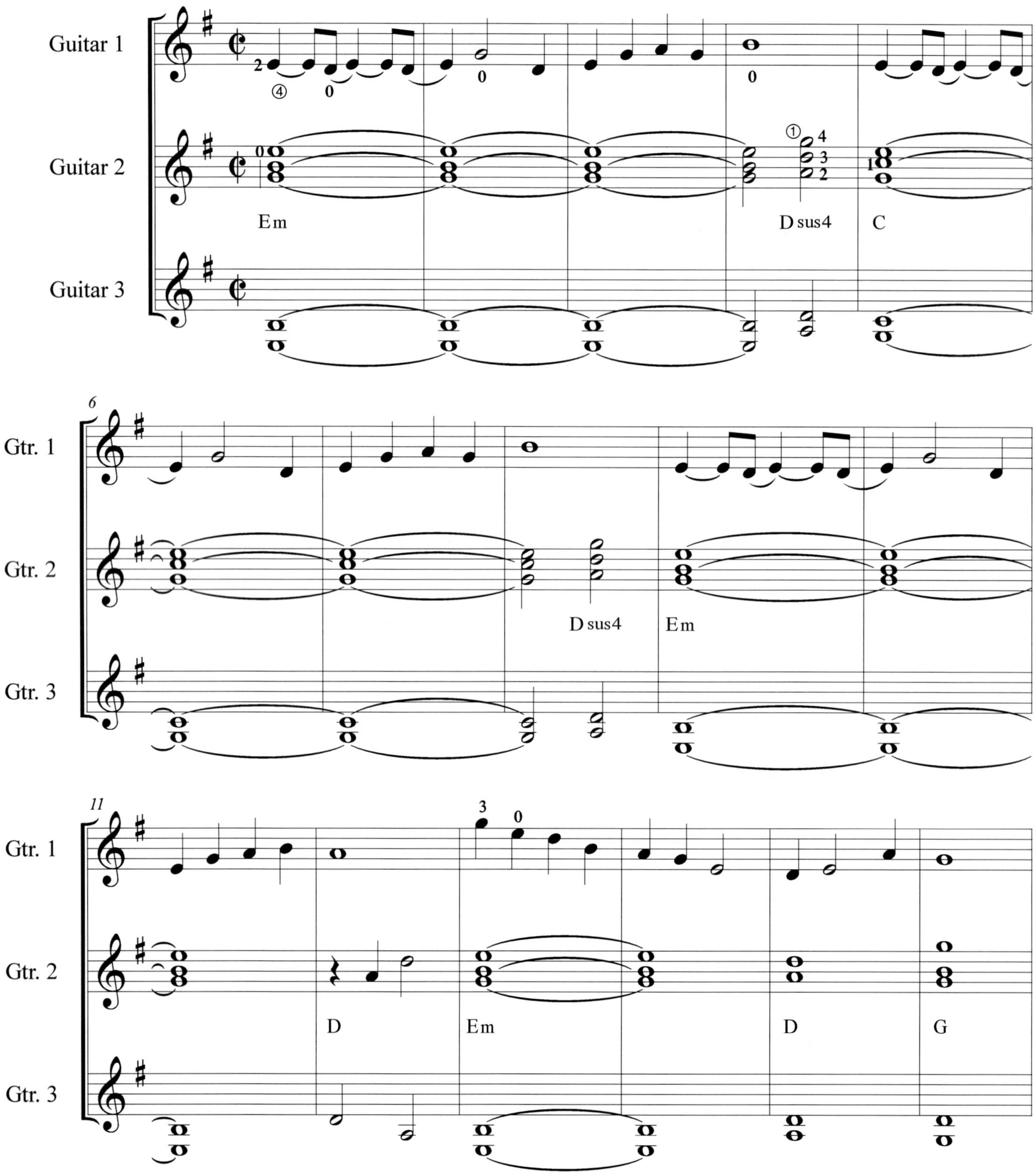

Guitar 1

Guitar 2

Em D sus4 C

Guitar 3

6

Gtr. 1

Gtr. 2

D sus4 Em

Gtr. 3

11

Gtr. 1

Gtr. 2

D Em D G

Gtr. 3

Students are surprised at how easy it is to play a cool riff after learning this tune. It is good for teaching hammer-ons, pull-offs and the open Em pentatonic scale.

17
Gtr. 1
Gtr. 2
Gtr. 3
Em
C
22
Em
27
B7
Em
D
G
D

33
Gtr. 1
Gtr. 2
Em
C
Gtr. 3
38
Gtr. 1
Gtr. 2
Em
Gtr. 3
43
Gtr. 1
Gtr. 2
D
Em
D
G
Gtr. 3
0
0
0

This page has been left blank to avoid an awkward page turn.

A Minor Twinkle

Traditional
arranged by Franco Bertucci

Faster is better

Guitar 1
Guitar 2
Guitar 3

Am | Dm Am | G F | E Am

Gtr. 1
Gtr. 2
Gtr. 3

Am G | F E | Am G | F E

Gtr. 1
Gtr. 2
Gtr. 3

Am | Dm Am | G F | E Am

Adding a drummer makes this piece even better.

13
Gtr. 1
Gtr. 2
(Chords repeat pg. 1)
Gtr. 3
17
Gtr. 1
Gtr. 2
Gtr. 3
21
Gtr. 1
Gtr. 2
Gtr. 3

Mode of Gloucester

Dramatically ♩ = 120

Franco Bertucci

Guitar 1

Guitar 2

Em

Guitar 3

5

Gtr. 1

Gtr. 2

B A B

Gtr. 3

8

Gtr. 1

Gtr. 2

B A G Em Em

Gtr. 3

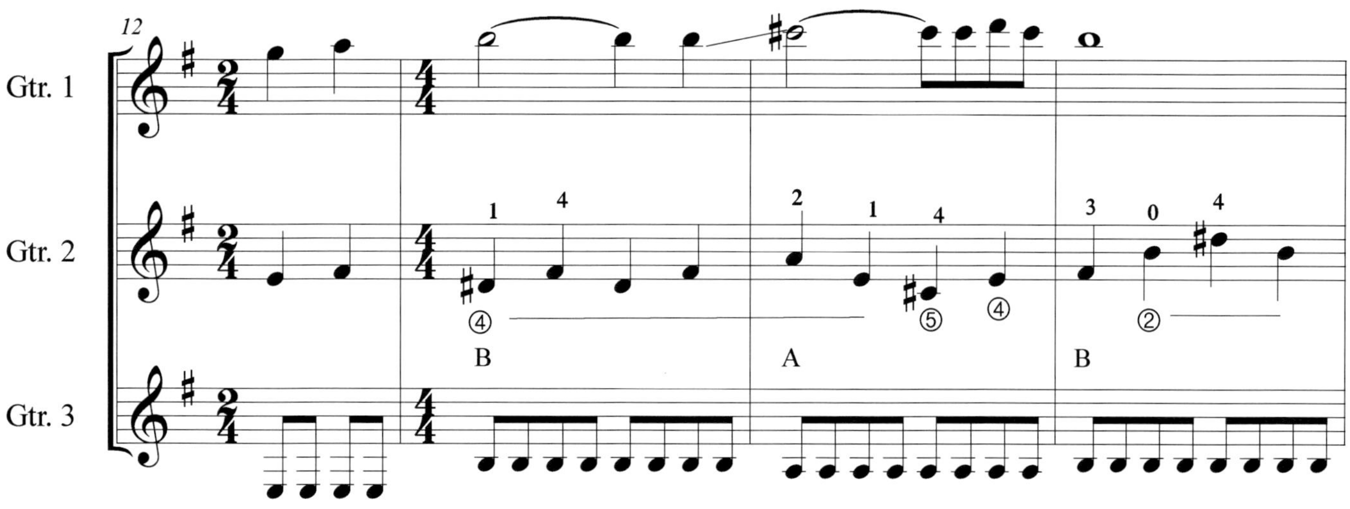
12
Gtr. 1
Gtr. 2
Gtr. 3
B
A
B

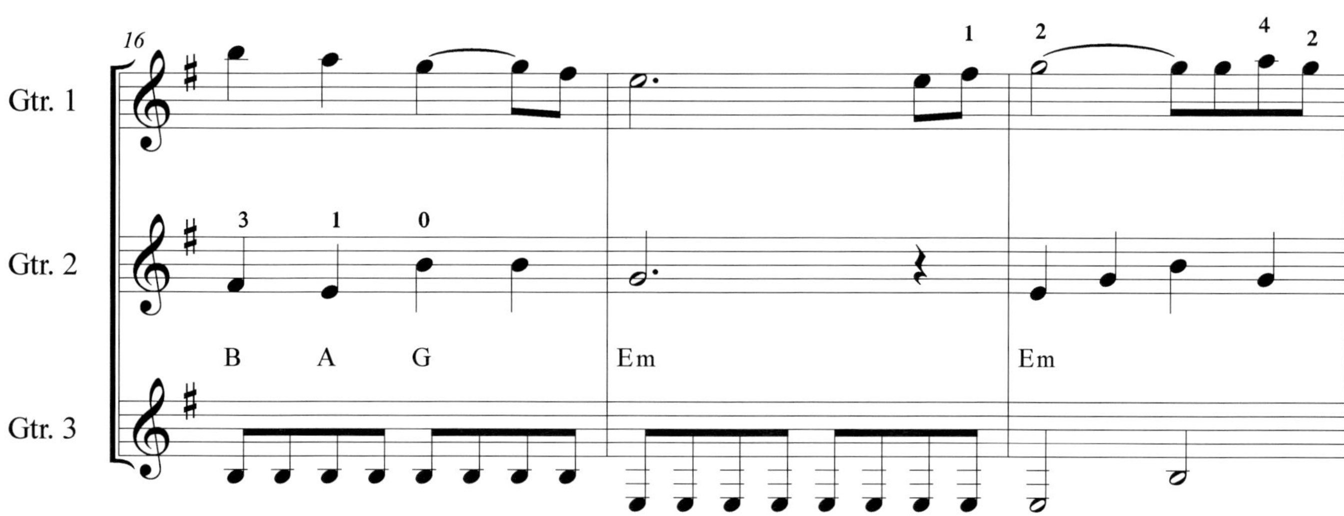
16
Gtr. 1
Gtr. 2
Gtr. 3
B A G
Em
Em

19
Gtr. 1
Gtr. 2
Gtr. 3
D
A
Bm

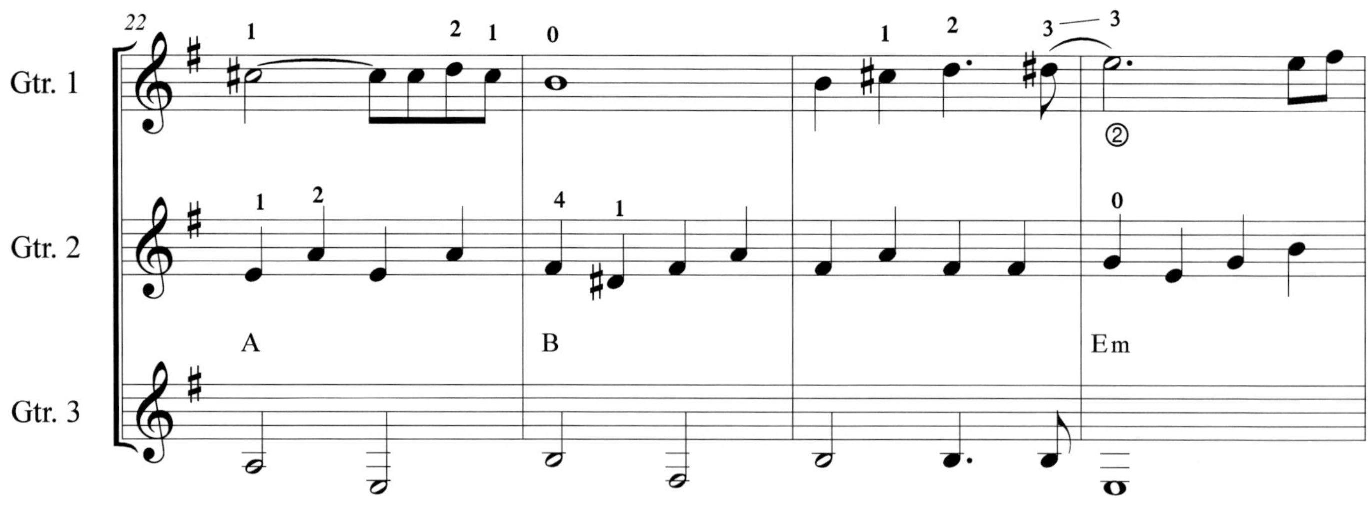
22
Gtr. 1
Gtr. 2
Gtr. 3
A
B
Em

26
Gtr. 1
Gtr. 2
Gtr. 3
B

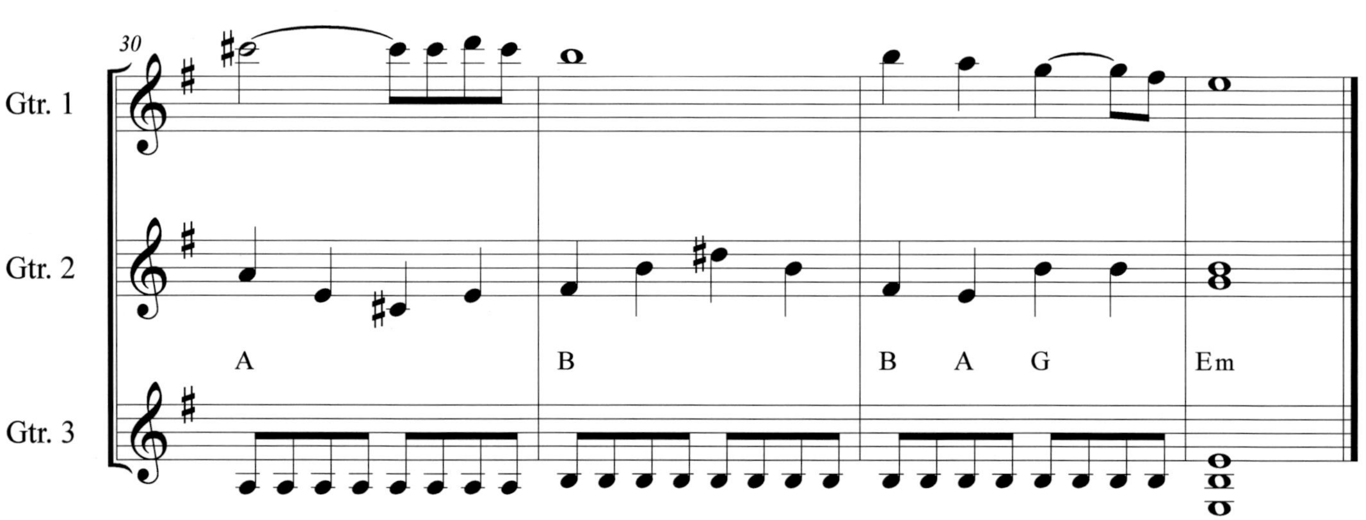
30
Gtr. 1
Gtr. 2
Gtr. 3
A
B
B A G
Em

About the Author

Franco Bertucci was a late starter. He began playing guitar at the age of 15, at which time he became completely obsessed with music. The piano was actually his first instrument, though he has spent more time on the guitar as it is more portable and practical for traveling bands.

His first teacher was folk musician, Beezy Taylor. She got him hooked by warning him never to become a professional musician. Franco then studied music and theater in college for two and a quarter years before running out of both money and the desire for a degree. He began to focus on writing and performing original music as a solo performer and with his band, Locust Street Taxi.

Over the course of a decade, he and the band gave over four hundred performances in ten different states and recorded several albums. Franco first began teaching guitar classes in the Pacific Northwest around 2012 when asked by the home school program, OPHC, of which his daughters were members. He has since taught music classes for both public and private programs and hopes to continue teaching, writing and performing music, wearing one hat or another, for years to come.

Other Mel Bay Recommended Guitar Books

13 Easy Trios for Guitar (Murdick)

American Patriotic Guitar Quartets (Petersen)

Beginning Baroque (Kiefer)

Beginning Pop/Rock Guitar Etudes (Douglass)

Christmas Music for Guitar Ensemble (Miller)

Dirt Simple Electric Guitar Solos on Open Strings (Nier)

Easy Way Christmas Guitar Folio (M. Bay)

Folio of Graded Guitar Solos (M. Bay)

Fun and Easy Solos for Guitar (Minamino)

Graded Guitar Duets (M. Bay)

Mastering the Guitar Duets (W. Bay/M. Christiansen)

20 Easy Classical Guitar Pieces for Kids (Eckels)

Early Music for Beginning Guitar (Boyd)

Easy Classic Guitar Solos (Castle/M. Bay)

Easy to Play Flamenco and Classical Guitar Solos (Hochman)

En Mode (S. Yates)

Etudes Mechaniques (S. Yates)

First Pieces for Classical Guitar by Louis Kohler (Griggs)

Graded Repertoire for Guitar, Book One (S. Yates)

Jorge Morel: Solo Pieces for the Young Guitarist

Duets for Beginning Guitar (Boyd)

Graded Guitar Duos, Vol. 1 (Small)

Jorge Morel: Duet Pieces for the Young Guitarist

Folk Song Collection for Guitar Ensemble (Hirsh)

Holiday Song Collections for Guitar Ensemble (Hirsh)

Hymn and Sacred Song Collection for Guitar Ensemble (Hirsh)

Jorge Morel: Quartet Pieces for the Young Guitarist

Music from Around the World for Guitar Ensemble (Miller)

Renaissance Dance Music for Guitar Ensemble (Hirsh)

WWW.MELBAY.COM